Doses of

Comfort

Daily Insights into Grief &
Suggestions for Healing

By Gwen Waller

Contents

Acknowledgments

Writing a book takes more than ideas and perseverance—it takes a team. I am so grateful for mine. Family members and friends have supported and encouraged me throughout the researching, writing and editing process. David, Katie, and Jessica, I especially appreciate the time you invested in reading this book and providing valuable feedback and input.

I'm also grateful for Mel and other bereavement professionals who officially trained me, as well as for the countless "teachers" who opened up their hearts, minds, and lives to me during their healing journeys. If I included their stories, I concealed their identities by altering names and details. Of course, I also learned through my personal losses, and I'm indebted to all who supported me during my own healing process.

Lastly, I want to acknowledge that *Doses of Comfort* has limits. It is intended to offer support and healing suggestions for those who are grieving, but it cannot address every situation or need. If your grief is inhibiting your ability to function in your family or workplace, please consult a professional counselor. And, however you proceed on your journey, be sure to give yourself permission to grieve, time to heal, and plenty of TLC.

Prescription for Healing

During a game of street football with our young sons and their friends, my husband ran to catch a pass and was taken down by the curb, which clearly favored the other team. He grimaced in pain as I drove him to a nearby clinic, where a nurse x-rayed and a doctor treated his broken arm. After weeks of immobilization and rehabilitation exercises, he regained most of his range of motion.

Years later, our family again benefitted from medical services. During a brief vacation at a friend's cabin, my son noticed a red spot on his leg. Given the setting, we all assumed it was an insect bite. The small bump grew into an expanding abscess, however, which seemed to be devouring his knee. Our doctor ran tests, which confirmed that our son had MRSA. Fortunately, the tenacious infection responded to a few rounds of powerful antibiotics.

I cringe to think of what would have happened had we ignored my son's infection or my husband's broken arm. Their bodies could not have healed properly on their own. Yet, after the loss of a loved one, we may try to disregard our pain and deny our need for healing. Perhaps we're embarrassed, afraid, or simply lack the energy to deal with our mental, emotional, and spiritual pain. Left untreated, however, grief tends to fester and eat away at our heart, mind, and soul. It can infect our relationships and interfere with our ability to function day to day. If we wait to address our pain, it is apt to become more complicated and require even more energy than if we had taken action early in our grief process. Also, those who initially rallied around us will most likely have gone on with their lives, so we will lack support for our delayed healing process.

Let's face it, being separated from someone we love hurts terribly; and hurts need healing. *Doses of Comfort* is designed to help you work toward that healing by taking a few moments each day or once a week to read and respond to one brief section. Consider it your daily or weekly dose of mourning. After reading each dose, you're invited to follow the suggestions that seem to fit your needs and situation. Warning: As your numbness wears off and you engage in the healing process, your pain may increase before it diminishes. This is normal. If you feel overwhelmed or in despair, however, please seek professional help. This book is not intended to be a substitute for grief counseling or other support.

After you read the entire book once, consider rereading all or portions of it to continue healing. The sections that were not as helpful your first time through may be more applicable the next time, because you'll be at a different place in your healing process. As you read and heal, be patient with yourself and also give yourself plenty of doses of self-care. Find ways to nurture yourself, as we'll address next.

Today's Dose of Comfort

What is one way you are experiencing your grief right now— what is one symptom of your pain? Consider starting a journal or confidential computer file for your grief journey, and begin to list the various ways this loss is affecting you. Keep this list in mind as you read on to discover healthy ways to work through your pain.

Get Plenty of TLC

In addition to taking time to mourn—to express our pain—it is vital to take time to nurture ourselves. Grief tends to deplete our energy and emotional reserves, leaving us feeling exhausted and empty. We promote healing by addressing our pain and giving ourselves plenty of TLC (tender loving care).

Just as individuals experience grief differently, we each benefit from various kinds of self-care. And our needs can vary from day to day. One day, curling up in a soft blanket and escaping into a good book may feed our soul. The next day, a brisk walk with a friend might relieve stress and encourage us. Most of us benefit from a balance of time alone and time with people who contribute to our sense of well-being. Complete isolation or a continual blur of activity seldom truly nurtures.

Taking care of ourselves also means saying "no" to people or activities that drain our limited reserves. Perhaps we can resume those relationships or commitments at a later time, but right now we need to protect our hearts, conserve our energy, and spend time with people who help nurture us. Though it may feel self-centered, our self-care will strengthen us and free us to be more attentive to others' needs in the future.

Today's Dose of Comfort

Write down at least ten activities that nurture you. Reading? Watching a movie? Exercising? Praying? Meeting a friend for coffee or a meal? Do at least a few of the options involve other people? Which one will you engage in today? Pick another for tomorrow, and consider scheduling one into every day this week.

Losses Come in All Shapes and Sizes

When we hear the word "grief," we usually think of the pain experienced after someone we care about dies. Yet we probably can name other losses and changes in our lives and relationships that have caused us to grieve. For example, since my brother's divorce, I miss seeing his ex-wife at family gatherings. When my husband's new job meant moving to another state, I grieved the changes in my friendships with neighbors. We no longer could share our hearts on morning walks or load all our kids into one of our minivans to take them on an outing.

We also can experience loss when we or our friends leave our workplace, organization, school, or religious community. Even if it was our decision, we may find ourselves grieving the relationships and the part of our identity left behind. While we might keep in touch through social media, texting and phone calls, we miss the intimacy of face-to-face interaction and the bond of a shared purpose.

Other sources of grief include infertility, physical ailments, disabilities, or financial challenges, which may dash our hopes and dreams. Unemployment, natural disasters, or betrayals can steal our sense of security. Even celebrated changes, such as graduations, promotions, and marriages, can include elements of loss, as the ushering in of a new season means the conclusion of a previous one.

Whatever the source or depth of our pain, our healing begins with acknowledging any losses and finding productive ways to express our feelings. Then we can begin to adjust and, down the road, even recognize and consider new opportunities resulting from the changes in our lives.

Today's Dose of Comfort

List the various losses that you have experienced during your lifetime, including moves, betrayals, divorces, unemployment, physical ailments, and other changes that have caused some degree of grief. Underline, circle, or put a star by the ones that have been the most painful. Can you identify ways that you've healed from and grown through your previous losses? What helped you through the process? If your pain has not diminished, consider applying the principles in this book to your previous losses, as well as to your more recent ones.

When Waves of Grief Hit

Not only do we grieve various kinds of losses, but any of those losses may resurface our grief for a loved one who died in the past. For example, moving may trigger our grief for the one who shared that house with us for many years. If our dog dies, we may find ourselves grieving not only the pet, but also the family member who brought him home and cared for him. Even a seemingly unrelated loss may remind us of a loved one we have mourned.

We also can experience waves of grief around holidays and other special occasions. On Mother's Day weekend, a surge may hit those without a mother and moms who have lost a child. As we anticipate or celebrate family weddings, graduations, and birthdays, we may find ourselves longing for those who are missing. If our relationship included certain activities, such as watching baseball, going fishing, eating out, or shopping together, then grief may strike as we cheer on a home run or visit the mall.

Sometimes waves crash upon us seemingly out of the blue. Several months after our infant son Darren died, I suddenly started to cry when I saw a helicopter. I hadn't even witnessed the hospital staff airlift my hours-old son to a neonatal unit across town. Still, seeing the helicopter triggered that memory and my longing for him.

Surges of sorrow also may result from hearing another's story or reading a book about grief, including this one. While conversations about loss may come at inconvenient times, we generally can plan when we will pick up a book. We can benefit from scheduling our reading when we can freely mourn.

Whenever grief hits, rather than trying to avoid or restrain the waves, we can choose to use them to help release our pain. We can allow the waves to help move us through our grief. If wave after wave is knocking us down and we fear drowning in our sorrow, however, it may be time to contact a qualified counselor or grief support group. Help is available.

Today's Dose of Comfort

If you're experiencing a wave of grief today, take a few moments to acknowledge your pain and embrace your memories. Then, just as swimmers are encouraged to use the buddy system, reach out to someone to assist you. Also take time to distract yourself from your loss.

Are you approaching a special day or activity? You might benefit from setting aside time to grieve (for further suggestions, see the Holidays and Other Special Days section at the end of this book). Also consider what you can do on that day to focus on loved ones who are still with you. If you suspect that a strong wave may hit you during a social event, prepare ahead of time by rehearsing what you'll say to others or by writing a note explaining that you were not up for staying. Then, if you feel the need to leave early, hand the note to the hostess or an understanding friend or family member before you go.

Expect the Unexpected

"So I'm not going crazy!" say members of grief support groups after reading a list of normal responses to grief. Hearing from others and learning about the variety of reactions to loss typically helps normalize the often frightening experience of grief. Without that reassurance, we may feel alarmed by and concerned about our feelings, thoughts, and physical symptoms. Learning what to expect after a death can provide some relief and comfort. Here are some—but certainly not all—possible responses to loss:

- Having more questions than answers
- Eventually finding peace with the questions
- Crying, weeping, wailing, sobbing
- One day catching yourself smiling (for real) and even laughing
- Being knocked down by a wave of grief when you least expect it
- A holiday or other day you dreaded isn't as bad as you anticipated
- Feeling like your heart truly has broken
- Someday realizing that, while you still have scars, your heart is mending
- Experiencing headaches, nausea, and other physical symptoms
- Feeling your pain intensify before it diminishes
- Struggling to get out of bed in the morning or to climb back in at night

- Losing your appetite or turning to food for comfort
- Wishing you could go back and change what happened, or at least say once more, "I love you"
- Replaying conversations with your loved one and finding comfort in hearing their voice in your mind
- Shaking your fist at God
- Reaching your hand out to God to carry you on this arduous path
- Reliving the pain of previous losses
- Finding hope in remembering ways you have healed from past losses
- Feeling like your grief is unbearable
- Being surprised that strength from within and support from without are enabling you to survive and heal

Today's Dose of Comfort

List some of the responses you have experienced so far on your grief journey. If any symptoms concern you, consult your physician or counselor. Also consider talking with or reading the stories of others who have experienced loss. Doing so can help normalize your own experience.

Here I Go Again

One day we may wake up feeling relieved, confident that we have completed the "anger stage" of our grief journey. A week later, however, we feel enraged. Or the numbness seems to have worn off, until we find ourselves again denying that this tragedy could have happened. We are confused, thinking we'd passed through one stage of grief, never to return.

Elizabeth Kubler-Ross ushered in a greater awareness of grief and loss through her writings on stages of grief: denial, anger, bargaining, despair, and acceptance. Many have assumed that all who grieve will complete one stage and then move to the next. Rather than graduating from one stage to another, however, we typically cycle through various reactions again and again. These responses may include, but are not limited to, shock or denial, anger, confusion, guilt, sadness, apathy, and fear.

Imagine holding a Slinky toy in your hand. As you pull it upward, the rings at the bottom stay closer together, while those toward the top are spaced apart. Similarly, early in our grief, our reactions to loss seem to be in a constant whirlwind. One moment we may experience disbelief that our loved one has died; later that day we may feel angry, as the reality of their death again sinks in. We might awaken feeling vulnerable, fearing our own or another's death, then spend much of the day confused, and return to denial by nightfall.

As time passes, the cycles spread out, like the top of the extended Slinky. Our grief reactions diminish in frequency and intensity. We certainly have not forgotten our loss, but the pain and its symptoms have lessened. Also, on our journey, we have learned coping skills for our various responses, which we can apply each time our grief resurfaces. Thus, through each cycle, we grow and heal.

Today's Dose of Comfort

Identify the ways you've reacted to your loss. What are you experiencing right now on your journey? Which coping strategies have been most effective when you've experienced responses such as disbelief, anger, confusion, guilt, or extreme sadness? Consider writing down your manifestations of grief and the healthy coping skills you've learned. Then, when those reactions cycle around again, you'll be prepared and better equipped to work through them.

Back to Normal?

In 1980, Mount St. Helens violently erupted, scorching 230 square miles of forest, and forever altering the landscape of Washington State. Afterward, the area impacted by the volcano appeared barren and lifeless. Before long, however, plants grew, animals returned, and new glaciers emerged. While Mount Saint Helens never will look the same as it did the day before the north face collapsed, it is a place of beauty, wonder, and geological study, admired by more than 300,000 visitors annually.

After the death of a loved one or another significant loss, we might feel devastated and long for life to be like it was before. Or our friends may ask us when our lives will get back to normal. Yet, as with Mount St. Helens, our loss has forever altered the landscape of our life. Rather than seeking to return to what once was, we heal and grow by establishing a new normal. We work to re-landscape our lives in light of our loss.

Our new normal may include redefining our roles, revisiting forgotten interests or cultivating new ones, and investing emotional energy in new or existing relationships. One widow, who enjoyed motorcycle rides with her husband, now exercises at the gym with her son. Another woman's Sunday routine had included calling her mom; since her death, she often calls another family member or friend that day.

As we rebuild our lives, we still cherish the memory of our loved one. But we also cultivate new relationships and interests.

In time, we discover beauty, meaning, and new life emerging from the ashes of our grief.

Today's Dose of Comfort

Reflect on the parts of your old normal you miss, and consider elements you want to include in your new normal. What are some activities you shared with your loved one? Are you ready to invite someone else to join you in that activity or in pursuing a new interest? Take your time as you rebuild and re-landscape your life; allow it to gradually grow and eventually flourish.

Why Are They Doing *That*?

After cancer took the life of their teenage son, Lydia felt the need to talk about her pain and weep. Certainly her husband would feel the same way, she assumed. Yet she looked out the window and saw Andrew chopping wood. Her pain intensified as she wondered, "Doesn't he care?" Lydia later understood that Andrew did indeed hurt deeply, and he was using physical exertion to work through his pain.

Just as friends and family members differ in their communication styles, love languages, and other aspects of their personality and relationship, they often differ in their grieving styles. Some may need to talk, cry, and journal their reactions. In other life situations, as well, they typically express their emotions outwardly and repeatedly talk about how they feel. In grief, this characteristic may intensify.

Other friends or family members may mourn by thinking and doing. Their lack of words or tears doesn't mean they don't hurt—they do! The loss may feel like a kick in their stomach. It also occupies their mind, as they replay the death over and over, trying to figure out what went wrong and how to make it right. Frustrated that they can't fix the death, they take other action. For example, after a teenager crashed her car through a fence and died, her grieving father longed to fix his daughter, but knew he could not. So he quickly went to work repairing the fence. After a young woman buried her mother, she initiated a fundraising run to support cancer prevention, hoping to help spare others from her pain.

In grief, and in all of life, we can heal and even help support friends and family members by recognizing and accepting our differences, as well as by expressing our own needs. Realize, too, that qualities that sometimes irritate us probably were among the attributes that initially attracted us to that person. Also, it is important to give ourselves and others the freedom to vary our grieving styles throughout our journey. At one point we may need to talk; later we may need to act, or vice versa. We—and others—are not limited to one style.[1]

Today's Dose of Comfort

What has been your most prevalent reaction to your loss? Do you feel the need to talk and cry? If so, take time today to share your pain with an understanding, supportive friend or family member, or journal your feelings. Many find it helpful to candidly talk with God through prayer. Also consider joining a grief support group. Sharing with others can help normalize your experience, and you may gain insights from their stories.

Are you more inclined to work out your grief through your thoughts and actions? If the same thoughts keep circling your mind, consider sharing them with someone you trust. Search the Internet for an organization that you can partner with to help prevent the kind of loss you've experienced, such as Relay for Life, MADD, March of Dimes, or the American Cancer Society. Find healthy physical releases for your grief.

If It Fits...

After our infant son died, one day I felt a strong urge to yell, "No!" I did not want to accept that Darren was gone! Not wanting our neighbors to be concerned and call 911, I sat in our van in our closed garage and yelled "No! No! No!" Releasing my anger and subsequent tears brought freedom and cleansing.

My reaction may sound strange to some, especially those who know that I typically remain calm in a crisis. But it fit the situation. After all, if a kidnapper had tried to take Darren, certainly I would have screamed, fought, and done all I could to hang on to him. So why shouldn't I want to yell in protest when death stole my son from me?

Too often, in our grief, we edit our responses, limiting the expression of our pain to actions we deem socially acceptable. Certainly we want to avoid doing anything that would physically or emotionally harm ourselves or another. But we need not stifle a feeling or reaction because we're not sure what others would think. Safely and freely expressing our pain often frees us from its hold on our mind and heart.

Today's Dose of Comfort

What could help you express your pain today? Some have vented by writing their feelings on fragile plates from a thrift store, then throwing the plates at a hard surface on a disposable tarp. Others have written messages on balloons and sent them heavenward. Adults, as well as children, have found comfort in cuddling with a soft stuffed toy, blanket, or pillow. Many have experienced healing through writing a letter to the deceased, expressing their love, forgiveness, sorrow, longing, and gratitude for what they shared together. Brainstorm ideas for expressing your grief, writing them down without evaluating them, even if they seem ridiculous. Then eliminate any ideas that could hurt you or another, and consider which activity you could try today or this week that could promote healing.

What Can Help Us Move Forward?

"You need to let go and get over it," you may have heard from a well-meaning friend. Yet we can't do either, and that is OK. Rather than "letting go" of our loved ones, we adjust our relationship with them and move forward. Rather than "getting over" their death, we move through our grief and adjust to a new normal, a revised reality.

To aid in this process, we may find it helpful to choose a linking object—something that reminds us of our loved one. It often is easier to move forward when we're taking with us a part of them or a token of our relationship. We might choose their necklace, ring, keychain, special pen, or a quilt made from their clothing. Keeping this symbol of their lives can help free us to take steps forward and invest in life and other relationships.

I often put on one of my mom's necklaces when I'm heading to a family gathering, and I'm usually not the only one who shows up wearing something that belonged to Mom or Dad. In this way, we honor them and acknowledge the impact they've had on all our lives. It feels like we're still including them in our celebrations. I also use my in-laws' serving dishes, which brings back warm memories of meals we shared together. As someone passes a platter, they might smile and say, "Remember when Granddad...," but we don't dwell on their absence.

We also can include loved ones in our future by evaluating and adopting some of their values and characteristics. How have they impacted us, and which qualities do we want to cultivate in our own lives? When we face a challenge, we may ask, "What would they say or do?" In these ways, we enable our loved ones to still be part of our lives without continuing to invest emotional energy into our relationship with them.

Today's Dose of Comfort

If you have not yet sorted through your loved one's belongings, consider selecting some items that are meaningful to you, which you could wear, use, or display. If you sew or know someone who does, consider creating a memorial quilt from their clothing. Or write a list of characteristics you admired in your loved one and decide if you would like to adopt or develop any of those qualities. Taking these steps can help you move forward on your grief journey.

Rebuilding While Healing

The day after my mom died, I had shoulder surgery. I certainly would have preferred to avoid both experiences, and the timing clearly was not ideal. Yet I knew that I could not ignore the impact of either, so I worked on healing and restoring my shoulder and my heart simultaneously.

At first, especially, I rested and protected my shoulder. I wore a sling, refrained from driving, and followed my doctor's other instructions. I also quickly started physical therapy. I saw my PT twice a week and adopted a rigorous routine of daily exercises. By devoting time each day to rebuilding my shoulder and to treating the injury with rest and ice, I eventually regained complete range of motion.

At the same time, I grieved my mom's death by working to mend my heart and rebuild my life. I cried and I worked through my pain by talking, praying, journaling, looking through photos, and helping create a memorial folder for my mom's service. I also distracted myself with books and movies, and I spent time with supportive friends and family. Since I no longer could talk and laugh with my mom, I invested my energy into other relationships. I organized and hosted family gatherings. In time, my heart responded to my efforts and nurturing care, and my new season of life-without-parents began to take shape.

Finding healthy ways to work through our grief while coping with the changes and restructuring our lives is called the dual process, as proposed by Margaret Stroebe and Henk Schut. As we simultaneously put energy into healing our hearts and rebuilding our lives, we are able to gradually move forward.

Today's Dose of Comfort

Take a moment to acknowledge your loss and verbally or physically express your pain in a safe way. Then consider how you can focus some of your limited energy on restoring and rebuilding your life without your loved one. What roles are now vacant that you or others can help fill? What activity or relationship would add meaning to your life? Consider reaching out to others in need, pursuing a hobby, or volunteering in your community. Also set aside time today for a healthy distraction from your loss—take a walk with a friend, read a novel, or watch a comedy. Keep nurturing yourself as you work through your pain and rebuild your life.

"It Can't Be!"

"You're kidding!" I blurted out. I knew my husband wasn't joking, yet my mind and heart wanted to deflect the words he had just spoken. It was nearly impossible to believe that a young friend, who seemed to have such a promising future, had ended his life.

Often our initial response to loss is shock, denial, and disbelief, which can manifest itself in various ways. In the fall of 1993, when the hospital staff told us our newborn son probably would not live, I shook involuntarily and was too confused to answer simple questions. During Darren's hospital stay, I remained in denial, as reflected in a family photo. I tried to wear a smile, while our four- and seven-year-olds' grief is unmasked. A week later, my husband and I both stood up and spoke briefly at Darren's memorial service, not because we were strong, but because we were numb.

Long after our loved one's death, we may still have moments of expecting them to call, text, or come through the front door. Or we might start to pick up our phone to call them when we need a listening ear or have exciting news to share. Perhaps we even set a place for them at the table.

Shock and numbness protects our hearts, minds, and souls in the first days and weeks after a death, but eventually we need to accept the reality of the loss. This is the first of four tasks of mourning identified by William Worden.[2] Our acceptance doesn't deny our wish that it wasn't true. And we may need to yell, "No!" in protest before we can admit, "Yes," in resignation. Nor does our acceptance negate the hope that we will see them again in heaven, which brings many people comfort. Working through the task of acceptance means that we intellectually and emotionally recognize that our loved one is indeed gone.

Worden calls this a task, because healing takes intentional effort and elbow grease. It also requires nurturing activities and self-care. As you work through the acceptance of your loss and Worden's other three tasks, which we'll consider in the pages ahead, continue to take breaks from your grief work. Give yourself—and allow others to give you—plenty of TLC.

Today's Dose of Comfort

What might aid you in gently accepting that your loved one has died? Rituals, such as funerals and memorial services, often help the bereaved face and begin to work through the reality of a loss. Honoring their life by giving time or money to a cause they cared about also is a means of acknowledging their death. If you find that you generally talk about your loved one in the present tense ("Bob is a practical joker"), consider switching to the past tense ("Bob was a practical joker"). If your loved one lived with you, are their clothes still hanging over a chair or their shoes by the front door? Your grief work might include moving these items out of sight or boxing up most of their belongings to eventually sort through and share with others who can use them. If the person who died always sat in the same spot at home or work, consider asking everyone to change where they sit, at least for awhile, as an acknowledgement of the deceased's absence. As you take steps to accept the reality of your loss, allow yourself to express the accompanying emotions and to receive love and support from others.

What's In a Name?

When I see an image of Martin Luther King, I hear his words echo: "I have a dream!" If someone mentions Mother Teresa, I immediately picture her "loving in-deed" and actively living her faith. When I think of my own father, I'm filled with gratitude for his hard work and generosity.

As you reflect on your loved one who has died, what words, phrases, or images come to mind? What characteristics or qualities helped define their lives? Were they generous, like both my parents were? Reserved? A mentor? Outgoing? Were they active in sports? Enthusiastic? Loving? An entrepreneur? Joyful? A teacher? Life of the party? Musical? A passionate volunteer? Athletic? Helpful? Talented? Hard-working? A practical joker? Organized? Faithful? An avid gardener?

Reflecting on who they were, how they lived, and what they meant to us and others is one way to acknowledge our loved one's death, as well as to honor their life and lasting impact. We can go a step further, and write their attributes in the form of a letter to the deceased or in a memorial acrostic. Through these and other creative endeavors, we can express our ongoing love and help keep their memories and legacy alive for us and for others, including future generations.

Today's Dose of Comfort

To create a memorial acrostic, write your loved one's name in a column down the left side of a page, as in the following sample.

You can use the first name, full name, or a nickname or title (e.g. Peggy, Grandfather, Junior, Coach, etc.). Then write a word or phrase that describes the person and starts with the letters of their name. With computer programs or calligraphy, you can craft a beautiful keepsake, suitable for framing. Photos of the loved one also can be included.

Consider making a duplicate for someone else who is missing this person. Perhaps you can give it to a friend or family member who shared experiences with you both. Or make a copy for a young child or grandchild of the deceased, who did not have as many opportunities to get to know them.[3]

In addition to honoring one who has died, we also can honor someone who is alive and well by creating a name acrostic, recognizing their interests, talents and qualities. Celebrating loved ones who are with us, as well as remembering those who have died, can facilitate the healing of our hearts and the rebuilding of our lives.

Remembering Gladys

Generous
Laughed a lot
Active in politics
Devoted to family
Yelled for her teams!
Sewed, knitted, crocheted, and tatted

Egyptian Story of Hope

When our infant son Darren died, I remember feeling like my heart truly had broken beyond repair. It seemed as if someone had strapped to my body an oppressive burden, which depleted my physical, mental, and emotional energy. At times my husband and I wondered, *Will the weight of our sorrow ever diminish?* Our grief felt overwhelming.

A story attributed to the Egyptians offers hope. It points out that when God created the world, he made everything small so that it could grow up with time. The grain grows into the wheat; the baby grows into the man; and the bud grows into the flower. Only sorrow was created full-grown, so that it might decrease with time, and we might be able to live with it.[4]

As the shock of our loss wears off, our sorrow intensifies. Then, in time, as we work through our grief, our pain will indeed diminish. We will not forget our loved one or the impact of their life and death—we always will treasure them in our heart. But our sorrow will decrease. In the process, our compassion, empathy, resilience, and faith most likely will expand. So, not only does our pain lessen and become bearable, but we ourselves grow in our capacity to live, love, and to respond to our own and others' sorrow.

Today's Dose of Comfort

Notice how the plants, children, and animals around you are growing. Remind yourself that, conversely, your sorrow eventually will decrease. Reflect on where you are on your grief journey and note any ways you already have seen your pain diminish. Have you also noticed an increased empathy for others? Envision what your life could be like in the coming weeks, months, and years as your sorrow decreases and your capacity for life increases.

Addressing Our Pain

In addition to accepting the reality of our loss (sometimes over and over again), we need to experience and work through our pain. This is Worden's second task of mourning.[5] We find healing as we identify our feelings and express them in healthy ways. We may work through our pain verbally by sharing our feelings with a trusted friend who can empathetically reflect back what we've said. Or we may prefer more physical expressions of our grief.

If we feel guilty about anything in our relationship with the deceased, we can write a letter, apologizing for hurts we caused and expressing forgiveness for wrongs we suffered. Though it will never be mailed, the act of writing can bring relief. We also may wish to share the letter with a confidant.

Anger can be expressed by throwing ice at the pavement, which requires no clean up, or tearing apart a phone book or cardboard box. Sadness can be released through tears. If we feel afraid, we benefit from naming our fears and considering how we've faced them in the past. Was our strategy effective? If not, how can we revise it?

For those with faith in God, we can take all of our feelings to him, as the Hebrew king David did throughout the Psalms. He openly expressed his anger, pain, guilt, and fears. Doing so helped him experience God's comfort and regain his perspective. I and countless others have found that this is still true today. After the death of our son, I ranted at God—it seemed so unfair! And I hurt so deeply. When I finished venting, I expected God's indignation, but instead I immediately sensed his loving presence and tender comfort.

As we face and work through our feelings—rather than running away, stuffing, or trying to numb our pain—we will experience healing and keep moving toward rebuilding our lives.

Today's Dose of Comfort

What is your primary emotional symptom of grief today? Guilt? Anger? Sadness? Fear? Or any of a myriad of other possible responses? Rather than keeping your feelings bottled up inside, safely express them using one of today's suggestions or other safe methods, including those found in the following pages. If your feelings seem overwhelming, consider meeting with a trusted confidant or grief counselor.

If Only...

After a loved one dies, we may wonder, *If she'd seen the doctor earlier, would she have been cured? What if he'd driven away five minutes later—would he have avoided the accident? Could we have done anything to prevent, or at least delay, the death?* We also may wrestle with regrets about the relationship. *If only I had spent more time with him. I wish I hadn't gotten angry over things that didn't really matter. If only I could have one more conversation with her.* We may replay various scenes, looking for ways to revise the story, because we don't like how it ended.

Normal responses to loss include guilt and regrets, which generally diminish with time and grief work, such as:

❖ Talking about our thoughts and feelings with a trusted friend, family member, or counselor.

❖ Remembering that no one is perfect, and that we probably did the best we could at the time.

❖ Writing a letter, expressing our regrets and guilt. Though we cannot send it to the deceased, we can benefit from this exercise.

❖ Being patient with and forgiving ourselves, our loved ones, and others.

❖ Focusing on what we did well in the relationship and the ways we expressed love and care.

❖ In light of our regrets, considering any adjustments we want to make now in our life and our relationships. This may include investing energy in helping others.

While we cannot revise past chapters, we have some control over future chapters of our lives. We can actively choose to seek healing and growth in the midst of our pain. We also can call upon God, who offers each of us grace, forgiveness, strength, peace, and hope as we live out the rest of our own life story.

Today's Dose of Comfort

If you've wrestled with "what if..." or "if only...," consider talking to someone or writing a letter to the one who has died, expressing your regrets, self-accusations, and feelings of guilt. Then evaluate your other relationships. Is there friction to eliminate or hurts you'd like to heal? Is there someone with whom you'd like to spend more time? Tell a friend or counselor, or list the efforts you plan to make to restore or improve these relationships as you write the future chapters of your life.

Mixed Emotions

It seemed as if we had lost my mother-in-law, Marilyn, years before she took her final breath. This once energetic woman who had loved to swim, golf, laugh, sing, and perform had lost her ability to communicate. She showed no signs of recognizing even Milford, her beloved husband of 63 years. Our hearts ached as her memory decreased and her anxiety increased. Eventually her body began to shut down, so we tried to keep her as comfortable as possible. In Marilyn's final moments, Milford sat by her side, tenderly holding her hand. Suddenly she released his hand and reached upward as she took her last breath.

Especially if death follows a long illness, as with Marilyn, we may react with mixed emotions. We may feel relief that they no longer are suffering, as well as sorrow at their absence. We might celebrate the years they enjoyed on this earth, as well as mourn that their life was cut short. If we believe in life beyond this world, we may feel sorrow at their absence and comfort in our belief that God welcomed them home and in our expectation of seeing them again with a whole mind and body.

Perhaps more difficult to acknowledge is the relief some people feel when someone who has hurt them dies. For years, they may have experienced the pain of neglect or abuse. If so, the bereaved may grieve deeply for what they missed during the person's lifetime, rather than because of the person's death. They may mourn the loss of their hope of ever having the relationship they longed for with the one who died. They also may feel greatly relieved, not because the deceased no longer suffers, but because that person who died no longer inflicts suffering on them and on others. Often this relief is accompanied by guilt and shame.

Have you experienced relief, for any reason, after the death of a family member, friend, acquaintance, or co-worker? Are you hesitant to accept and express some of your thoughts and feelings? You may wonder, *What will people think?* You are wise to be cautious; it not advisable to share everything with everyone. But you can promote healing and freedom by confiding in a trusted individual who recognizes that death often is followed by a complex mixture of thoughts and emotions.

Today's Dose of Comfort

List the various reactions you've experienced after this death. What aspects of the relationship are you grieving? If you feel some relief, list the reasons why. Consider sharing your list with a trusted confidant, such as a close friend, family member, mentor, spiritual leader, or professional counselor.

What About Anger?

Late one afternoon, about two months after our son Darren died, I could feel my anger welling up inside of me and spilling out onto my family. I was short-tempered with our other sons, but I knew I wasn't really angry at them. I was mad at death! It had stolen our infant son from us. I talked with a trusted friend, which helped, but I needed to do more. So I asked her to watch our boys while I took my tennis racket and balls to a nearby school playground. With each slam of the ball against the wall, I released some of my rage toward the enemy death. I returned home, freed from the power of my anger, and only a little sore in my shoulder.

Anger is a common and natural response to death. After all, we have been robbed—deprived of continued time on earth with someone we love. As a result, we may feel anger toward a drunk driver, medical personnel, family members, God, friends, the deceased, or ourselves. Whether or not any of these targets merit our fury, it is important to find safe ways to express it. This can include talking to an understanding friend, family member, pastor, or counselor; journaling; exercising; hitting or screaming into a pillow; or whacking tennis balls.

After finding a healthy release for our anger, we may feel exhausted. We can benefit from taking time to nap or to curl up with a good book or movie. Throughout our grief journey, it is vital to not only express our feelings, but also to nurture ourselves.

Today's Dose of Comfort

Take your anger temperature by completing this sentence: "Today I feel _____." (Possible responses include but are not limited to: frustrated, annoyed, ticked off, angry, furious, enraged, and irate.) Then ask, "Am I misdirecting my anger at myself or others, or am I expressing it in healthy ways? Have I identified the true target of my anger?" If you're feeling any degree of anger, consider expressing it to someone you trust. If that provides no relief, further explore the source and meaning of your emotion. Also consider journaling, exercising, or finding another safe way to work through your feelings.

Facing Fear

In a perfect world, all of our children would outlive us and our spouse would remain by our side as we raised our family and then doted on our grandchildren. Each family member and friend would live a long, healthy life. In this relational utopia, we would enjoy many decades of gathering for holiday meals, riding together to sporting events, exploring new restaurants or vacation destinations, and sharing in other activities.

Clearly, we do not live in a perfect world, and the death of a loved one may have shattered whatever hopes we had for our future. It feels like our world has been turned upside down, especially if death struck without warning or took the life of one who barely had a chance to live. We tend to feel vulnerable, afraid of what might happen next. What other changes or losses are lurking around the corner? Death has heightened our awareness that we cannot control everything in our lives or count on others always being there. We also face our own mortality.

After our son Darren died, I tried to calm our other sons' fears while dealing with my own. We all felt more vulnerable. One day, I successfully resisted being overprotective and allowed seven-year-old Brent to join his cousins on a carnival ride that seemed to swing into the clouds. With my eyes glued on him, I prayed for his safety while strategizing how I would catch him if he flew out of the seat. I'm thankful to report that we both survived his ride.

During our grief journey, we can move toward healing by expressing any of our anxieties and considering what has helped us face our fears in the past. We also might ask ourselves, "What is the worst thing that could happen? How likely is it? If it transpires, what could I do and who could help me through it?"

Many people find that prayer and meditation on God and his faithfulness eases fear. Belief and trust in One who is loving and powerful can bring peace of mind as we work through our grief and face the future. In addition, focusing on the blessings of today can increase our joy and diminish our worries about tomorrow.

Today's Dose of Comfort

Take a moment to express any fears and acknowledge your blessings. Then consider what you can control on this earth. Have you adopted a healthy, safe lifestyle? Are you prepared for possible tragedy in the future, though it is unlikely? Schedule a time to prepare or update your health directive, power of attorney, and will. If you have young children, consider who you could entrust them to if you were to die.

If your children are expressing fears regarding the future, you may wish to assure them that you are taking care of yourself and plan to live a long life, but if anything ever happens, you have carefully selected guardians to lovingly meet their needs. Addressing these concerns is not easy, but it generally will ease your mind and theirs.

Forgiving Someone Who Has Never Apologized

Carl still doesn't know who murdered his teenage daughter, Ali, more than a decade ago. Each time a possible suspect is identified and DNA is tested, the agonizing memories resurface and a degree of healing work must be repeated. Yet, despite the recurring pain, Carl has been able to forgive this faceless man who extinguished the life of his precious daughter.

For some, like Carl, healing from grief includes forgiving someone who caused a death, whether intentionally or accidentally. This might include a drunk driver, careless doctor, or the deceased themselves. Others grapple with forgiving the one who died for the ways they inflicted pain on others during their lifetime. In either case, forgiveness is a process, which takes intentional work and time.

As with other aspects of our grief work, forgiving another starts with our decision to seek healing. Do we want to hang on to the hurt, which weighs us down? Or are we ready to release it? If so, our first step is to acknowledge our pain and even our hatred of the one who harmed us. As author Lewis Smedes writes, hatred is a natural response to someone who has inflicted deep pain, and it often coexists with our love for that same person. Hatred may be subtly lurking within us, draining us of healing energy; or it may be aggressively rearing its head with a longing to lash out, which often damages our other relationships. Either way, it hurts us more than it hurts the one we hate.[6] So we benefit from identifying our hatred and moving toward healing.

Once we have acknowledged the evil that was done and our subsequent feelings, we begin the next step. We turn our eyes away from our wounds and look with new eyes at the one who hurt us. Without denying any atrocities they committed, we recognize that they, too, have hurts and needs. Rather than seeing them as all or mostly evil, we see them as human—as we are human—with a mixture of faults, good qualities, and their own unmerited wounds. [7]

If we are forgiving someone who died, we cannot restore our relationship with them, but we can alter their ongoing influence in our lives. No longer do we see only or primarily the pain they inflicted, but we also recall the attributes we loved and admired. We edit our memories to focus on their humanness and positive qualities.

If, like Carl, we are forgiving someone we may never meet, we move through these steps without seeking restoration with the betrayer. Yet, within our own hearts and mind, we are restored and freed from the weight of hatred. Carl thanks God for helping him experience this and other aspects of his healing. He certainly will always miss his daughter, but he's able to pray for her killer without asking for vengeance. He even can wish him well, which Smedes would say is evidence of his forgiveness.[8]

Today's Dose of Comfort

Did someone come to mind as you read about forgiveness? Consider sharing any feelings, including hatred, with a trusted confidant or writing them in letter form. Don't hold back your anger. Then, when you're ready, turn your focus toward that person's neediness and imperfect humanness, and even their positive qualities. Make efforts to begin moving to that place where you can wish them well.

Adjusting to Their Absence

After the death of a loved one, our life changes dramatically and never will return to "normal." So we work to create our new normal. We put effort into Worden's third task of grief,[9] which is adjusting to our altered environment. As with the other tasks, learning to live without our loved one is not a one-time act, but a process.

To facilitate this adjustment, we consider all that this person meant to us and did for us. What obvious and subtle roles did our loved one play, and who can fill those voids now? What other relationships have changed as a result of their death? We examine our needs and consider how they can be met. This process is likely to resurface our pain, so it is vital to keep identifying and expressing our thoughts and emotions, as well as to take breaks from our grief work and nurture ourselves.

For one widow, adjusting to life without her husband has meant starting a new career so she can provide for her family. Another has learned to mow her lawn and is pursuing new interests and friendships to help meet her emotional needs. Children who have lost a parent often help care for younger siblings, as well as take on household chores and annual traditions, such as putting up Christmas lights. They also may deepen their bond with a teacher or other adult in their life to help fill the void. After Grandma dies, an aunt, uncle, or grandchild may begin to plan family gatherings.

While no one else can ever replace our loved ones, we adjust to their absence by looking to others or ourselves to help meet the needs they once met.

Today's Dose of Comfort

What are specific ways you are aware of your loved one's absence right now? What parts did they play in your life, and has anyone stepped into those roles yet? Generally, one person cannot take on all their responsibilities, so consider which roles you or others can meet. This may mean hiring someone to complete certain jobs, relying on others to help meet your emotional needs, and leaving some roles vacant for now. For example, if your deceased spouse always planted a vegetable garden, but it is not a priority for you, perhaps you will choose to let the land rest at least for a season, ensuring you have time to take care of yourself.

Remembering and Honoring

"Would you like to buy some cookie dough?" a third-grader asked. As I flipped through the fund-raising catalog, I saw much more than cookie dough and a vast myriad of food and gifts. I also saw reminders of my mom's generosity and thoughtfulness. If she was still alive, I suspect she would have bought the wrapping paper on page 15, even though she hadn't even opened several packs she'd purchased from her grandchildren. No doubt, she also would have ordered 10 chip clip sets—one for every household in the family. We would find them in our stockings next Christmas.

What activities or images tend to resurface memories of your loved one? When you watch a football game, do you miss him yelling at referees or jumping out of his seat after a touchdown? Do certain songs make you smile as you can almost hear her renditions at karaoke nights or singing together around a campfire? Perhaps, as you drive past someone walking their dog in a downpour, your heart warms with thoughts of your loved one's devotion to their pets.

As you catch their reflections and revisit your memories, consider the impact this person has had on your life. How has their life influenced your values, knowledge, beliefs, or self-esteem, whether positively or negatively? Which aspects of their lives would you like to emulate? Which traits or habits do you hope to avoid?

Evaluating how a person's life has influenced ours in the past can help us be more intentional in how they affect us now and in the future. We can choose to move away from traits we consider undesirable and strive to carry on the aspects of their legacy that we value. Doing so can bring comfort to our hearts and greater meaning to our lives.

Today's Dose of Comfort

List some of the ways that the deceased has impacted your personality, beliefs, values, and habits. Do any of your attitudes or actions remind you of them? How do you feel when you find yourself acting like them? Which characteristics from their life would you like to abandon? What aspects of their influence would you like to retain and develop in your own life? Select a trait from their life that you deem positive, and consider one way you can express it this week. Carrying on their legacy can facilitate your healing and growth, as well as honor their memory.[10]

Who Am I?

After her husband's death, Marie felt lost without her role as George's wife. For twenty-nine years, he had been her companion, lover, and closest friend. As his health declined the past five years, she had willingly devoted most of her waking hours to his care. Now what?

One of his parents died suddenly and the other succumbed to a long illness before Rick's thirty-second birthday. When friends referred to him as an adult orphan, he shook his head. He didn't like that label, but he felt confused about who he was and where he belonged in his altered world.

A dad and mom were devastated when their young adult son tragically died. Now, two years later, they were burying their only remaining child. In the midst of their pain, they wondered, *Are we still parents?*

Death not only steals our loved ones, but also can alter our roles and raise questions about our identity. If we had invested most of our time and energy into that relationship, we might feel insecure and displaced after their death, like a boat drifting without an anchor or destination. Individuals who have cared for a disabled child or an ill parent or spouse are especially vulnerable to these feelings. Death not only has taken a person they treasured, but it has eliminated a role that consumed much of their time and energy. Confused, they wonder who they are and what they do now. Like someone who has been "laid off" from their job, they might feel insecure and inadequate.

Acknowledging our loss and redirecting energy into our remaining roles can help us adjust to our altered world. This might mean spending more time with other family members or friends, strengthening those ties. We may choose to invest time in new relationships by volunteering at a school, church, or nursing home. We also might sharpen our career skills or expand our education.

For some, investing in other roles takes great effort. One widower with no children acknowledged that he and his wife never sought other friendships because they enjoyed each other's company so much. Suddenly Ted felt completely alone. Though it took most of his limited energy, he reached out and began to build friendships and pursue new interests. As a result, he was able to expand his identity and rebuild his life after the death of his beloved and constant companion.

Today's Dose of Comfort

List your various roles in your family, profession, organization, neighborhood, and community. Are you a father or mother? Teacher? Friend? Neighbor? Aunt or uncle? Member of the Rotary Club or a church? A volunteer at the food bank? Artist? Mentor? Student?

Next, draw a circle on a piece of paper or find a white paper plate. Divide the circle into pie-shaped wedges, one for each of the roles you listed plus one for the relationship you had with the deceased, as in the sample that follows. Write that role in one section (which you may wish to make larger than the others), and add a few words or pictures illustrating what you enjoyed most about that role. Then, in each of the other sections, write another role and a few details about what you enjoy about it. If you have difficulty coming up with current identities, write down roles you could actively pursue. Include at least one step you could you take to move into that role.

After completing your circle, cut out a wedge-shaped piece of paper and tape the outer edge to the rim of the circle, so it covers your role with the deceased. Tape only one side, so that you can still lift the paper and look at that section when you wish. Notice that, while it hurts to have lost that part of your identity, you have other remaining roles and relationships. Now read what you wrote about those aspects of your life. Circle or put a star on any roles you would like to focus on or strengthen at this time.

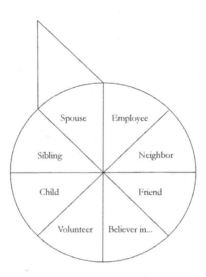

Reinvesting In Life

Sue, a young widow, had continued to wear her wedding band on her left hand, as well as her husband's ring on a chain around her neck. One day, however, she sensed that it was time to remove her ring. At first, she slipped it on the chain with Will's, but it felt heavy. Sue realized she needed to remove both rings and acknowledge her uninvited singleness. This was a significant step in withdrawing energy from her relationship with her deceased husband and rebuilding her life. Sue, who later remarried, still remembers and loves her first husband. She and her second husband, Jack, who also was widowed, remember and talk about their first spouses. They honor the ones who died, without idealizing or comparing them to one another, and they help their children remember their deceased parent in appropriate ways.

As we work through our grief, our goal is certainly not to forget our loved one. We will long remember them and the relationship we treasured. To heal, however, we consciously withdraw emotional energy from the deceased and reinvest in life. This is Worden's fourth and final task of mourning.[11]

Some resist this task because they feel like they're abandoning or betraying their loved one. They continue to focus much of their energy on the deceased, which can impede their relationships with the living. Yet, the healing and rebuilding process requires us to gradually divert our attention from the one who has died, so we have more energy to reinvest in life.

This might mean taking fewer trips to the cemetery and spending less time in the deceased's room or gazing at their photos. We may choose to return to activities we had shared with the one who died, perhaps inviting a friend to join us. Or we might pursue new interests. Reinvesting in life often includes reaching out and finding ways to help others. Most likely, we'll need to start slowly and continue to schedule in doses of mourning and ample self-care.

Once we've worked through Worden's fourth and final task, we may hope for a diploma from the School of Mourning. But since grief recycles, we are likely to find ourselves repeating each of these tasks in the future. If we look back on the first steps of our journey, however, we'll see that we're at a different place and our hard work is producing healing, growth, and renewal.

Today's Dose of Comfort

Carefully consider how much emotional energy you're investing in your relationship with the deceased. Then determine one way you can divert some of that energy and reinvest in life this week. Perhaps you can sign up for a class to grow in your knowledge or skills and to meet new people. Or participate in an event that supports a cause that is close to your heart. Simply meeting someone for coffee and talking with them about how they are doing might be your first step.

Write Way to Heal and Rebuild

While there's not a "right" way to mourn and rebuild, one effective method is to write down our thoughts and feelings. As we've seen throughout *Doses of Comfort*, journaling can be a safe avenue for expressing our anger, admitting our fears, and working through our pain. The act of putting words on paper or on our computer can help us identify and process the various grief responses that may be churning inside us. In black and white, they generally become more manageable and productive.

In addition to helping harness the power of thoughts and feelings, writing can be a means of contemplating our future. We can brainstorm options for rebuilding our life. Does our loss necessitate a job change or move? We can list the possibilities. If we've been caring for a loved one, which interests or relationships have we put on hold? Do we want to revisit any past hobbies or endeavors? Which new interests could we pursue? Perhaps we'd like to learn a new language, try oil painting, or run in a 5K.

Another healing strategy is writing a letter to the deceased. Even though we cannot send it to them, the act of conveying any regrets, anger, longing, and other responses to loss can bring healing in our own life. If our relationship ended with unfinished business, we can apologize for our actions and express forgiveness for wrongs we suffered. In addition, we may find it freeing to share our plans for reinvesting in life, including our hesitations as well as our hopes. Of course, letters also can be a way to thank them for cherished memories and articulate the love that still fills our heart.

Whether we keep our written expressions private; disclose them to someone we trust; or read them to God, the act of writing down our thoughts, feelings, and options for the future can promote healing. Doing so can be a constructive step toward rebuilding our life without our loved one.

Today's Dose of Comfort

If you have not already done so, consider buying an attractive journal in which to write your thoughts, feelings, and hopes for your future, or start a confidential computer file. Later you may want to share some or all of what you write but, for now, keep it private so you can write freely, without fear of being criticized or misunderstood. If anything you write alarms you, however, or if you feel overwhelmed with emotion or troubling thoughts, reach out to a friend, pastor, or professional counselor.

"What Time Is It?"

"To Everything (Turn, Turn, Turn), there is a season (Turn, Turn, Turn), and a time to every purpose, under heaven. A time to be born, a time to die..." [12] This song reached number one on the Billboard Hot 100 chart when the Byrds recorded it in 1965. Inspiration for the lyrics, however, dates back nearly 3,000 years earlier, to the biblical book of Ecclesiastes. "There is a time for everything...a time to weep and a time to laugh, a time to mourn and a time to dance."[13]

Clearly, these truths are timeless. After the death of a loved one, however, we may have difficulty turning from tears to laughter, from mourning to dancing. We may allow ourselves to cry, but feel guilty when we laugh. Perhaps we are concerned that others will measure our love for the deceased by counting our tears. We may fear that our levity will discount our devotion.

Yet, most likely, those who have died would want us to do all we can to take pleasure in life now. They would encourage us to embrace our experiences of delight as well as our surges of grief. Rather than asking us to try to prove our ongoing love for them, they would want us to remember all the ways we showed love to them while they were here with us.

Tina recognized this after her sister, Rachel, lost her battle with cancer at age 50. Tina missed her sister and the frequent phone calls that often left them doubled over with laughter. She knew that Rachel's husband and daughter, Nicole, were grieving deeply, too, so she invited them to visit six months into their healing journey. The trip provided ample doses of hugs, tears, and laughter, as they all shared stories about Rachel. Then, knowing it would lift both their spirits, Tina surprised Nicole with a parasailing trip for her twenty-first birthday. She even brought along some of Rachel's ashes, as a way of including her in the adventure. Certainly, Tina and Nicole were missing Rachel, but they were able to turn from their pain and literally rise above their circumstances as they laughed and celebrated Nicole. No doubt, Rachel was smiling from heaven.

Of course, parasailing isn't for everyone, but we all will benefit from embracing and even pursuing joy during this season. Healing transpires as we not only set aside time to express our feelings of grief and loss, but also take time and allow ourselves the freedom to smile, laugh, and find pleasure in life. After all, there's a time for everything.

Today's Dose of Comfort

When was the last time you watched a comedy or read a book that made you truly laugh? Today might be the day to seek relief through humor. Consider asking someone to join you. Have some tissues close by, as you may find that laughter releases some of your tears.

Have you smiled lately? If not, is it because your heart is still too heavy, or are you refraining because you do not feel free to express any degree of happiness? Consider giving yourself the gift of freedom to smile today. Even if your heart is heavy, try to share a smile with someone else who could use it. Smiles and laughter not only promote healing—they're also contagious.

Being Nurtured by Nature

During every season of grief, we benefit from allowing nature to nurture us. This includes taking time to smell the roses...or gardenias, lilac, sweet peas, magnolias, and lavender. Maybe even bring a bouquet inside. Buds and blossoms can cheer our hearts and renew our hope. They remind us that, though leaves fall and die in autumn and many trees appear lifeless in winter, their beauty is renewed in spring and summer. Similarly, though the landscape of our personal world has changed we, too, can experience growth and renewed life.

Other aspects of nature also can strengthen and refresh us. We can find joy in seeing hummingbirds and bright tanagers, as well as in listening to song birds. Watching a seagull, hawk or majestic eagle soar can remind us that we, too, will rise above our circumstances. Basking in the warmth of the sun can encourage our hearts, and rain can help cleanse our minds. In winter, the silence of a snowfall can quiet our minds. On any clear night throughout the year, we can regain perspective as we gaze into the vast heavens.

Much of nature is beyond our view and understanding, but that need not keep us from finding peace in its presence. In fact, the mysteries of life might help us face the mysteries of death. Even though we live with unanswered questions regarding our loss, we can experience hope and peace as we focus on the visible beauty and seasonal renewal of nature.

Today's Dose of Comfort

Take time today to relieve stress by taking a walk outside, soaking in the sights, smells, and sounds. Notice beauty that you may have overlooked before. If you believe in God as the creator of all that surrounds you, reflect on what nature reveals about him and how those attributes can help you trust him. Also consider bringing a bit of nature inside by picking or buying flowers or a cheerful plant.

Ongoing Expressions of Love

When those whom we treasure die, our love for them lives on. That's one reason that loss hurts so badly. They no longer can express their love to us, and we no longer can express our love to them. We can, however, find ways to express our love *for* the ones we miss.

After a loved one dies of cancer, many people choose to donate, walk, or run to express their continuing love, as well as to raise money to save others from that disease. Those who have had a life stolen from them because of alcohol or drugs might donate money to organizations working to prevent drunk driving or to centers that treat alcoholism and drug addiction. A mother or grandmother whose arms feel empty after the death of a baby may volunteer to hold infants or nurture needy children. Adult children who have lost parents can express their ongoing love by visiting lonely seniors.

Throughout the years since the death of our son, parents, and friends, we have expressed our enduring love in various ways. When our other sons were younger, we all wrote messages on a helium balloon and then released it heavenward to Darren. One year, at the anniversary of his death, we donated toward efforts to bring clean water to South Sudan, with the hopes of preventing the deaths of infants, children, and adults there. This year, I am writing this book in his memory. We also have supported life-giving causes in honor of our parents.

Sharing our ongoing love for the ones we miss can help us find meaning in their life and death, which can lessen our pain and facilitate our healing.

Today's Dose of Comfort

Since love is a verb—an action—consider what you can do this month to express love for the one who has died. Were they passionate about a particular cause and, if so, do you want to invest time or money in it? Are you drawn to support organizations that are striving to prevent others from suffering the same kind of death that claimed your family member or friend? Perhaps you would find it meaningful to spend time with someone in need. Write down possibilities that come to mind, and be open to other ideas and spontaneous opportunities to express your continuing love.

Learning From Life's Storms

One January, freezing rain hit Western Washington and nearly paralyzed the area in which I live. Large ice-covered branches snapped, taking down power lines, and roads resembled ice-skating rinks. More than 200,000 people lost electricity, some for nearly a week. The thaw brought continued danger and damage as heavy ice chunks dropped from trees. Schools and many businesses shut down, and people were urged to stay home. As we looked out our windows and witnessed the power of nature, we were reminded that much of what happens in our world is beyond our control. But we can determine how we will respond to adversity.

At our house, when the ice storm left us without electricity, we ran our portable generator part of the time. It provided minimal power, however, so we left off most lights and used one appliance at a time, and only when truly necessary. Similarly, while grieving we have limited physical, mental, and emotional energy. Generally it is best to curtail our activities and be selective as we invest time in relationships. Which friends or family members understand our pain and will nurture, rather than drain, us? We promote restoration by conserving our energy and protecting ourselves.

Washington's ice storm also provided a picture of resilience. Branches of tall roses, blueberry bushes, and other plants were encased in ice, which caused them to bend low, many touching the ground. As the ice gradually melted, however, the branches straightened and were restored, ready to bear flowers and fruit in spring and summer. In the midst of our grief, we may feel like those plants, weighed down by sorrow and nearly breaking. Yet with time and in a healing environment we, too, are restored and experience new life.

As we begin to rebuild our life, we are wise to plan ahead for future storms—for losses we may face down the road. Preparation includes doing our part to protect and maintain relationships, quickly repairing breaks, and frequently expressing our love. We also are wise to carefully consider what we believe about life on earth and life after death, and why we hold those convictions.

Today's Dose of Comfort

To promote restoration after loss, consider how to expend your limited energy. Which activities and relationships will enhance your healing process? Take a look at your calendar for the coming week and month. Are you exhausted just looking at your commitments? If so, consider what you can cancel or postpone. Whenever possible, write your plans in pencil and give yourself permission to protect yourself and conserve your energy. In time, as you regain strength, you gradually can increase your level of involvement and productivity.

As you begin to restore and rebuild your life, consider ways you can prepare for losses you may face in the future. Are any of your relationships strained and, if so, what steps can you make toward restoration? Also, while it is unpleasant to face your own mortality, have you protected your family by creating an advance directive and will? Most importantly, are you prepared spiritually? Those who are confident they will spend eternity with God experience peace and hope as they face their own inevitable death, as well as comfort during seasons of grief.[14]

Spiritual Perspectives on Loss and Grief

When our son Darren lingered between life and death, a friend gave me a card with a simple, heartfelt message that became my lifeline. Diane clearly knew something of my pain, having buried her stillborn daughter four months earlier. She also knew God's comfort. So she shared with me the promise that was keeping her afloat: "The Lord is close to the brokenhearted and saves those who are crushed in spirit" (Psalm 34:18).[15]

Diane was right. I especially experienced this reality the night I poured out to God my broken heart, my confusion, and my anger—the unedited version. I held nothing back. Then, realizing I had no right to be enraged with the Lord of the universe, I waited for the lightning bolt to strike. It never did. Instead, I sensed God's gentle, loving presence and comforting embrace in a way that defies description.

I later realized that God hates death more than I do. The Bible says, "The last enemy to be destroyed is death" (1 Corinthians 15:26). "He will destroy the shroud that enfolds all peoples, the sheet that covers all nations; he will swallow up death forever. The Sovereign Lord will wipe away the tears from all faces" (Isaiah 25:7-8). Then, God will rebuild, according to his perfect design. He "will create new heavens and a new earth....Never again will there be in it an infant who lives but a few days, or an old man who does not live out his years" (Isaiah 65:17, 20). Someday, no hearts will be broken by the pain of separation.

In the meantime, God understands. When Jesus walked this earth, he grieved deeply, knowing this world is not yet as it should be. He openly wept for his dear friend Lazarus, even though he was about to raise him from the dead. If God in the flesh mourned, certainly grief is a normal, natural, healthy response to loss.

Thankfully, we need not grieve alone. God, who understands our pain more than we ever will, longs to walk with us, comforting us. He is "the Father of compassion and the God of all comfort, who comforts us in all our troubles, so that we can comfort those in any trouble with the comfort we have received from God" (2 Corinthians 1:3-4). He knows, he cares, and he is near. If we embrace his comfort, eventually we can even help comfort others, as my friend Diane did.

Today's Dose of Comfort

If you have entered into a life-giving relationship with God through Jesus Christ, take time today to find comfort in his presence. He can handle your questions, fears, anger, tears, and anything else that plagues you. He hopes that, in exchange, you will receive his comfort, peace, and love. His arms are open wide.

If you do not yet know God, consider seeking him now. Our Heavenly Father is no stranger to grief, as he allowed his only son to die on the cross for all of us. Though excruciating for both Father and Son, they willingly suffered so that we could be cleansed and have a relationship with God. And they both knew that Jesus would rise from the grave, thus experiencing and offering us victory over death. If you have not yet accepted God's gift of forgiveness and life, he invites you to call out to him. He longs to comfort you now and express his love to you for all eternity.

Doses of Comfort for Specific Losses and Seasons

When Children & Teens Grieve

Megan was five years old when her dad died in a tragic accident. She initially responded by sticking to her mom like Velcro, fearing that she would suddenly lose her, too. Now, nearly ten years later, Megan's greatest concern is that she will forget the father she barely knew. So, though she loves her mom's new husband dearly and cherishes their father-daughter relationship, she is the only family member who refers to him as her "stepdad," rather than "dad." In this way, she protects her relationship with her father. Megan's parents also help preserve his memory by sharing stories of Dad and together watching home movies of her early childhood.

Like adults, children have different grieving styles, but their responses also are influenced by their developmental stage. From about age two to seven, a child might see death as reversible and ask when the deceased will be back. From four to eleven, they may blame themselves because in a moment of anger they'd wished the person was dead. It also is common to ask questions over and over again. Children may suffer from nightmares, become apathetic, withdraw from friends, and have difficulty concentrating at school. Regression is common for preschoolers through preteens.

Grieving teens often repress their anger, mask their depression, and deny other emotional responses to their loss. They hesitate to talk with other family members who are hurting, as they don't want to add to their pain. Besides, as teenagers, their job is to increase their independence, so it goes against their grain to reach out to adults for support. Parents and teachers might remain oblivious to the teen's inner turmoil, and thus maintain high expectations for grades and post-graduation plans. Tragically, teens without a trusted confidant and healthy release valves for their pain and pressures often turn to alcohol and drugs, act out sexually, drive recklessly, or engage in other dangerous activities.

Not surprisingly, when children and teens grieve, the adults in their lives may not recognize their pain and expressions of grief, let alone know how to help them. If those adults are grieving the same loss, they may feel unable to comfort them, due to their own intense pain. Or, if the child or teen is grieving the death of a peer, the adults may minimize the impact of their loss.

How can grief-stricken adults support children and teens? Encourage younger children to talk and draw pictures pertaining to the loss and their grief. Invite them to tell you about their pictures, which may provide insight into their inner world. Answer questions honestly but carefully, as they do not need to know every detail. Address their fears. Children often wonder if they'll die next. Or will their parent die and, if so, who will take care of them? While no one can promise they'll always be there, parents can offer reassurance that they're doing all they can to live a long life and to keep the child safe. They also can explain that, though it's very unlikely, if the parent ever could not take care of the child, a relative or friend would. Also, strive for as much consistency as possible, which contributes to their sense of security, and help them keep alive the memory of the one who died, as Megan's mother and stepdad wisely have done.

Help teens find a trusted confidant, perhaps a school counselor, youth pastor, or grief counselor. In some communities, churches or nonprofit organizations offer support for grieving children, teens, and families. Teenagers— as well as children and adults—need safe expressions for their anger, fear, confusion, and sorrow. If possible, tune in and listen when they offer a glimpse into their mind and heart. Avoid trying to quickly "fix" their pain or control them, but instead reflect back what you hear and encourage their healthy verbal and nonverbal expressions of mourning. One mother knew not to push her son to talk about his feelings, but recognized that he was processing his pain by creating a DVD of his dad's life.

If your family draws hope and strength from your faith, help your child and teen confide in God, sharing all their feelings. You also can point them to assurances offered by your spiritual beliefs. Avoid saying, "God took them home" or other phrases that might confuse a child or cause resentment toward God. (Review Spiritual Perspectives on Death for insights into how God feels about loss.)

Whenever possible provide grieving children and teens with consistency, acceptance, empathy, and comfort, remembering that they're on a journey, too.

Today's Dose of Comfort

How are the children and teens in your life responding to the loss you are grieving? Watch this week for expressions of their pain, no matter how subtle. You need not be perfect in how you respond to their words or actions, but strive to be present with them in their grief. Also, search the Internet for grief support options in your community, which you might utilize now or in the future, if needed.

Traumatic Death

"I'll bet you didn't see this coming," a teenager wrote in his suicide note. He was right—his parents were shocked...and devastated.

Others have been stunned to open their front door to a chaplain, whose eyes began to tell the story before he spoke the words no one wants to ever say or hear. "There's been a terrible accident..." or "He was involved in a fight, and...."

I once met a widow who lost one husband suddenly and another after a long illness. She readily admitted that both experiences were excruciatingly painful, yet also had some distinct differences. Others agree. When death is anticipated, we generally enter the grief process earlier and have time to reach out and try to repair any breaks in the relationship. We also may have a chance to say good-bye. Because our loved one has endured a long period of suffering, we may experience some relief at the time of death, and then grieve more deeply later. When death is sudden and traumatic, however, we have no time to prepare, so our shock and other reactions tend to be more intense.

Even after a traumatic death, the initial shock helps protect us from experiencing the full force of the pain at once. Early in the journey, we may go back and forth from disbelief—this is a terrifying nightmare—to being hit hard with the reality of the death. Our grief may include flashbacks of what we saw, if we were at the scene of the death, or of what we imagine happened, if we were not.

As the reality of our loss settles in, our emotional responses may intensify. If our loved one died by suicide, we might feel angry and even enraged that they ended their life. In our sorrow, we may have a deep longing for more time with them, as well as sadness for the despair that tormented them. Our stomach and neck may be tight with anxiety, as we wonder who else in our world is feeling hopeless and considering suicide. We also are apt to try ourselves in the courtroom of our mind. If so, we owe it to ourselves to make it a fair trial. Rather than just accusing ourselves with our regrets and perceived failures, we also need to cite the evidence of how we expressed love for the one who died. We ought to avoid judging ourselves and others harshly, realizing that, for reasons unknown to anyone else, at the moment the person ended their life they saw no other way out of their pain. It is not our fault.[16]

Guilt also can plague us after a fatal accident if we think we had any influence over them being on the road at that time, whether or not we did. If they were impaired by alcohol, drugs, exhaustion, texting, or other distractions, we may search throughout the history of our relationship for any way we could have prevented the accident. When the deceased is at fault, and especially if others were harmed or killed, we also may feel ashamed and hesitant to talk about our loss, let alone our personal pain.

Yet, as is true for all grief journeys, after a traumatic death, it is vital to find healthy ways to express any of these and other normal responses. Talking to family members, friends, a pastor, a counselor, or in a grief support group can help us work through our pain and find healing. We may need to retell, over and over again, the story of how we first heard about the death. While a death might happen suddenly, our healing takes extended time, conscious effort, and patience with ourselves and others.

Today's Dose of Comfort

If you're grieving a suicide, accident, or other sudden and traumatic death, write down or talk to a trusted family member or friend about how you first learned of the death. Who told you and how? What were your first thoughts? Then write or talk about what you felt when you heard the news, and what you are feeling now. Don't edit your responses—share your experience, even if you're embarrassed or think your feelings don't make sense. Lastly, focus on pleasant memories of your loved one and make a plan for taking care of yourself, especially now.

Consider seeking out a support group in your area specifically for those who have experienced this type of loss. See the Additional Resources section of this book for more information.

Holidays and Other Special Days

Some ocean waves appear ominous as they approach the shore, but then hit the sand with little force. Similarly, you may find that the anticipation of holidays or other significant days is worse than the day itself. At other times, you might not expect a wave to hit, so you are caught off guard when it slams into you. The following considerations and additional Doses of Comfort for Special Days at the end of this section may help you prepare for occasions that might elicit grief surges.

Birthdays, Wedding Anniversaries, and Anniversaries of Their Death

During the first year after our son died, the monthly anniversaries of his birth and death seemed to intensify my grief. Sometimes I was conscious of the dates; other months I wasn't aware of the date until my mind would start replaying hospital scenes. My husband usually wasn't thinking about the monthly anniversary, but often would notice a wave of grief sneaking up on him during that time. After the first year, the monthly responses diminished. However, we have continued to remember and honor Darren's life and lasting impact on the yearly anniversary of his quick journey to heaven.

For some people, dates are significant grief triggers; for others, they are not. Have you noticed if you typically are aware of the anniversaries of your loved one's birth and death? There is no right or wrong answer, nor is there a correct time or way to honor loved ones who have died. If you choose to remember them on the anniversaries of their birth or death, consider the various suggestions contained throughout this book or one of the suggestions listed at the end of this section.

Birthdays and Weddings of Family Members Who Are Living

Birthdays and weddings are joyous occasions, but you also might be especially aware that someone's chair is empty. If you are planning your own wedding, consider whether or not it will be helpful and meaningful to acknowledge the deceased in any way during your ceremony. It should be your choice—not other family members' decision. Some have found comfort in placing a flower on the seat the loved one would have occupied. Others have lit candles or read a scripture or poem that was significant to their loved one. Many choose not to do anything that day.

Likewise, at any age, on birthdays you might miss a loved one who typically would have called, sent a card, or celebrated with you. You may benefit from talking briefly with someone who is also grieving this loss or will empathetically listen. Also consider spending a few moments looking through photos of past birthdays. These activities can help prepare you to celebrate your own life and enjoy those who are honoring you on your birthday.

Christmas

Anna knew there was no way around that first holiday season without her husband, so she determined to get through it by being intentional. Some family traditions were maintained; others were put aside, at least for that year. Instead of their typical trip to the Christmas tree lot, she drove her children to the mountains to cut down a tree and play in the snow. When they got it home, the eldest son stepped into Dad's role of putting on the lights and all the children decorated it. The children insisted on including Dad's special ornaments. On Christmas Eve, they again broke tradition. Instead of gathering with family, they went to the Christmas Eve service at church, and then out to eat. Being intentional and preparing for the holidays helped reduce Anna and her family's stress and manage their grief.

Becky's father had died three months before Christmas, and her mother's health was failing. She had hoped that her siblings could set aside long-standing differences and celebrate the holidays together. Other family did not feel the same way, so Becky consciously chose to lower her expectations. She moved beyond her disappointment and found freedom in focusing on enjoying her husband, adult children, and mother.

Depending on your situation, consider the following holiday suggestions or the Doses of Comfort for Special Days at the end of this section.

> ❖ Evaluate your traditional "to do" list, which might include decorating, baking, shopping, sending

Christmas cards, and/or entertaining. Ask yourself, *What can I skip this year? What would I like to revise for at least this season? Which traditions do I most want to include this year? Who could I ask to help me?*

❖ Permit yourself to change your mind about attending a holiday celebration or to leave early if a surge of grief hits. You may wish to write an explanatory note ahead of time, which you can leave on the counter or give to your host as you excuse yourself.

❖ Give yourself the gift of TLC. Listen to your body and meet your needs for rest, refreshment, nutrition, and nurture. Also give yourself time to release your emotions through tears, talking, journaling, exercising, looking at photos, or engaging in other healing activities.

❖ Remember your loved one by giving a gift in their memory; buying a special ornament; hanging a Christmas stocking for written memories or expressions of love; and/or lighting a memorial candle, which you might place by a framed photo.

Planning ahead and taking care of yourself can help you find comfort—and even joy—during the holidays.

Valentine's Day

After Christmas, retailers generally waste no time lining the shelves with Valentine gifts, cards, and candy. You may find yourself surrounded by beautiful bright red hearts, yet yours feels broken and shattered. Your love for the deceased lives on, yet they are not here to give and receive your love or tokens of affection.

As with all special days, there is not one correct way to respond. Some who recently have been widowed have found it healing (though also painful) to buy a Valentine card for their deceased spouse and write words of gratitude and love. Others choose to avoid their store's greeting card section altogether, as it tends to open the floodgate for their tears. If they traditionally sent cards to other family members, they realize they have to shelve that tradition for at least this year.

The first Valentine's Day after our infant son Darren died, our family chose to decorate empty cereal and cracker boxes, which we then placed in our kitchen. Throughout the month, our then five- and seven-year old sons, my husband, and I wrote or drew simple messages for one another and dropped them in one another's boxes. We found encouragement in opening our boxes each day and seeing a lopsided heart drawing, "I miss Darren, too," or "I love you."

If you anticipate that Valentine's Day will intensify your pain, consider which healthy coping strategies might promote your healing and comfort. Also look for others in your community who have experienced loss. Make the effort to reach out to them for support. In the process, you're likely to help ease their pain, too.

Easter

One spring, Easter and the one-year anniversary of my dad's death landed on the same day, so our family gathered to remember both. We carried on some of our Easter traditions, and also shared memories of my dad as we divided up his hat collection among his children and grandchildren. Years later, the second anniversary of my mom's death fell on Good Friday, and I was mindful that both days were significant to my parents. Jesus' death for our sins, as commemorated on Good Friday, and his resurrection to new life, as celebrated on Easter Sunday, gave my parents hope and courage to face their own deaths. They knew that when they died physically, they immediately would be fully alive with their Risen Savior.

For Christians, the cross is the primary symbol of Easter, yet it is not the only one that can encourage the bereaved. Another is the Easter lily. After its bulb lies hidden and dormant through the long, cold winter, a strong plant emerges, stands tall, and blooms. New generations of bunnies, ducklings, and chicks also remind us of the continuing circle of life. And Easter eggs symbolize the seed of new life. These and other aspects of Easter can encourage us that we, too, will experience renewal and restoration after loss.

This year, in what ways will you celebrate the hope of Easter? You may want to write down or share with someone the evidence of renewal you have already seen in your own life. Also consider bringing an Easter lily or other flowering plant into your home in memory of your loved one and in recognition of your growth. If you are trusting in Jesus' death and resurrection, you can find hope and comfort in knowing that in heaven you will be reunited with your loved ones who believed, as well as with your beloved creator and Lord.

Mother's and Father's Day

In May and June, it is difficult to avoid the store aisles of Mother's Day and Father's Day cards and street corner flower vendors. Then turn on your TV and, before you can mute it, you are likely to hear sentimental background music while a parent patiently bakes cookies with their child (and sells flour or other essential ingredients). Another commercial will bring you face to face with a grateful young adult teaching their parent to use the cell phone they just unwrapped. For those who have lost a child or parent, Mother's Day and Father's Day can heighten awareness of their absence or reopen the wound. Depending on where you are on your grief journey, consider the following healing activities.

- ❖ Write a card or letter, expressing your ongoing love and what you miss about him or her. You also may want to recall a memorable time together and thank them for what they have meant to you and how their influence continues. This letter can be kept private or shared with a family member or friend.
- ❖ Plant a tree, shrub, or flower in memory of your loved one.

- ❖ Evaluate your loved one's impact on your life. Which qualities do you admire and hope to carry on? Which characteristics would you prefer to abandon? Also consider who else you would like to influence your life.
- ❖ Encourage someone else to be all they are meant to be.
- ❖ Ask a nearby nursing home if you can spend time with a resident who rarely has visitors.
- ❖ Call or visit someone whose heart may be aching on these special days.
- ❖ Donate to an organization that helps children in need around the world.

During Mother's Day, Father's Day, and other special occasions, take time to remember those who have died, and then focus time and energy on people who are in your life right now. Let them know how much they mean to you, and spend time enjoying them.

Memorial Day

For some, Memorial Day weekend means camping, gathering together for barbeques, or catching up on spring yard work. For others, it is a time to reflect on the sacrifices of loved ones and others who have served our country. In our home and countless others, it is both.

Whether or not they died during a war, we can honor the memory of soldiers by visiting their graves or other memorials. You might find it meaningful to drive through a National Cemetery on Memorial Day weekend, where flag after flag line the road, saluting those who have served.

Generally, on Veteran's Day and Memorial Day our family chooses to display the neatly folded United States flag presented to us at my father-in-law's interment. Another Stars and Stripes waves proudly outside our house. Sometimes we look at photos from the war and recall stories of the bravery and selflessness of our fathers and grandfathers. We acknowledge the price they paid and the emotional scars they carried through their lives after the wars. Often on these days, we ask God to protect the men and women serving now and to give wisdom to those leading our military forces. We also pray for peace—in our world and in the hearts of all who grieve.

Honoring the memory of loved ones can help us heal and move forward. It also is vital that we make time for self-care, including relaxation and recreation. On Memorial Day weekend, consider reflecting on those who have served and taking time to relax and build new memories, which can bring you and others joy now and in the future.

All Saints' Day

A few months after my dad died, our family went camping. As I sat near our tent, gazing at the lake, I heard voices nearby. A high school team was using the campground as a track. When the first runner crossed the finish line, I heard a few cheers. The volume and energy steadily increased as she and those who finished behind her lined the road to urge on every last runner. "Come on! All the way through!"

I smiled as they called out to their weary teammates. How wonderful to be supported like that! I felt like even I could run a great distance with such camaraderie. Then I remembered that we have an even greater number cheering us on from heaven as we continue on life's journey.

In November, All Saints' Day is an opportunity to be encouraged by the lives and lasting legacy of those who already have finished the race of life. Consider taking time to reflect on family members and friends who loved, served, worked, persevered, and trusted in God. Whether or not you are a Christ-follower, you can be inspired by saints from the Bible— Noah, Moses, Ruth, David, Daniel, Mary, and Paul—as well as more recent saints, such as Abraham Lincoln, Martin Luther King Jr., and Mother Theresa.

Imagine if you could hear their voices, cheering you on. What would they call out to you? On All Saints' Day, and any day, the legacy and memories of your loved ones can encourage you to run "all the way through."[17]

Thanksgiving

For many in the United States, Thanksgiving is a day for counting our blessings and gathering together to eat, eat, and eat. Depending on where we are on our grief journey, however, our pain may cloud the view of any blessings in our life. Our loss also is likely to diminish our appetite for food and socializing. We may dread the thought of trying to carry on the same traditions without our loved one.

As time passes, our pain lessens, but we may still experience smaller waves of grief during the holidays. As with all seasons of our journey, we can move toward healing by acknowledging and expressing our pain. Then we can continue to rebuild our lives by giving thanks for the ways our loved ones have impacted our lives. Consider listing ways you have been affected by your loved one. Have you adopted some of their characteristics, values, habits, or traditions? Did they teach you life lessons? By acknowledging our losses and anything we've gained through our relationships and experiences, we can continue to heal and rebuild our lives.

Though feelings of gratitude may not come easily right now, make conscious efforts to look beyond your loss to see the gifts and blessings you still have. Consider listing the people who are in your life now and the ways they influence you and contribute to your life and well-being. If your family gathers for the holiday, consider taking time to share together positive memories of the deceased and to express gratitude for their life, as well as for the lives of those who surround you now.

Doses of Comfort for Special Days

In addition to the suggestions above, consider the following ways to promote healing and to help rebuild your life.

❖ Before a special gathering or situation, mentally rehearse what you will say or how you will respond to questions about your loss.

❖ Prepare one of your loved one's favorite meals or desserts.

❖ Listen to one of their favorite songs.

❖ Plant something in your yard in their memory.

❖ Give to a food bank or charity in their memory. You cannot bring back your loved one, but your gift can help improve the life of someone else.

❖ Reach out to someone who is lonely or in need.

❖ Gather with others who miss the deceased. Add water to a small vase until it is about one quarter full. Then pass the vase and a small bowl or basket of floral stones or flat glass marbles. Invite each person to drop in a stone as they share a memory of the loved one. When everyone has shared as many memories as they like, or as time allows, point out that, just as the stones fill the vase, our memories fill our hearts. Also notice that the water level has risen, reminding us that our hearts have expanded through our grief.[18]

❖ Create a scrapbook and fill it with memories of your loved one, using photos, postcards, event programs, and other keepsakes. Include written descriptions, highlights, and stories of your times together. Or incorporate your memories into a digital photo book.

❖ Next to a framed photo of the deceased, place a candle (battery or flame) and light it when you are especially missing them.

Closing Thoughts & Additional Resources

Now that you have read *Doses of Comfort*, consider rereading all or portions of the book as your grief continues to cycle. Because you will be at a different place in your healing journey, you may find some insights and suggestions more applicable than they were the first time through. Be patient with yourself as you continue to heal and rebuild your life in the absence of your loved one. And remember to give yourself plenty of doses of TLC.

To find further support for your healing process, contact your doctor, pastor, local hospital, or school counselor. Many medical centers and churches offer grief support groups or can refer you to local resources. You also can find information and support on the following websites. These national grief and loss groups may have a local chapter in your area.

Organizations Supporting the Bereaved:

Grief Share www.griefshare.org

The Compassionate Friends: Supporting Family After a Child Dies www.compassionatefriends.org

Survivors of Suicide www.survivorsofsuicide.com

Also by Gwen Waller

Finding Comfort in God's Embrace: 31 Meditations for Those Who Grieve, 2005, available at Amazon.com.

Notes

---

[1] For more information about grieving styles, see Kenneth Doka and Terry Martin's book *Grieving Beyond Gender: Understanding the Ways Men and Women Mourn* (New York City: Routledge Imprint, Taylor and Francis Group, 2010).

[2] For more information on the Tasks of Mourning, see William Worden's *Grief Counseling and Grief Therapy: A Handbook for the Mental Health Practitioner*, 4th Edition (New York City: Spring Publishing Co., 2009).

[3] I first found the idea for a memorial acrostic in *Our Story* by Mel Erickson, © 2002, Erickson ISBN 0-9716782-1-9. This book contains several healing activities for children and has been used extensively in grief support groups, as well as by individuals.

[4] This Egyptian Story appeared on a handout for *GriefWorks*, which formerly served the bereaved in Washington, and was attributed to a New York chapter of The Compassionate Friends.

[5] See Worden, *Grief Counseling and Grief Therapy*

[6] Lewis B. Smedes, *Forgive and Forget: Healing the Hurts We Don't Deserve* (San Francisco: Harper and Row, 1984), 21.

[7] Ibid., 27.

[8] Ibid., 29.

[9] See Worden, *Grief Counseling and Grief Therapy*

[10] To further explore how a loved one has impacted your life, see Dr. Robert Neimeyer's **Lessons of Loss, A Guide to Coping**, (Memphis:Center for Study of Loss and Transition, 2006), p.149-151.

[11] Worden

[12] "Turn! Turn! Turn! (to Everything There is a Season)," lyrics by Pete Seeger in the late 1950s, recorded by the Byrds in 1965.

[13] Ecclesiastes 3:4, NIV

[14] God has revealed himself through the world around us (he is more beautiful, powerful, and complex than his creation); through the Bible (my all-time favorite book); through his son, Jesus Christ; and through people, who reflect his image (though imperfectly). If you do not know God personally, I encourage you to ask God to open your eyes to see him and your heart to experience his love. Talk to him, sharing your questions, doubts, fears, and longings. I also invite you to read the gospel of John in the Bible, taking note of the ways Jesus describes himself. I believe that he loves every person and longs for a close relationship with them, just as we long for an ongoing relationship with the people we love.

[15] All Scripture quotations are from the Holy Bible, New International Version®. Copyright 1973, 1978, 1984 by International Bible Society. Used by permission of Zondervan. All rights reserved.

[16] For more information about suicide loss, see John Jordan and John McIntosh's *Grief After Suicide: Understanding the Consequences and*

Caring for the Survivors (New York City: Routledge Imprint, Taylor and Francis Group, 2011).

[17] "Since we are surrounded by such a great cloud of witnesses…let us run with perseverance the race marked out for us" (Hebrews 12:1).

[18] This exercise, which has been used with all ages, is adapted from *Teen Talk: A Grief Support Group for Teenagers* by Nanette Flynn and Mel Erickson, ©2000 GriefWorks, p. 61.